NATIONAL GEOGRAPHIC
GEOGRAPHIC INVESTIGAT
INVESTIGATES NATIONA
ES NATIONAL GEOGRAPH
GEOGRAPHIC INVESTI
IC INVESTIGATES NATIO
ATES NATIONAL GEOGRA
AL GEOGRAPHIC INVES
HIC INVESTIGATES NAT
IGATES NATIONAL GEO
ONAL GEOGRAPHIC INV
RAPHIC INVESTIGATES N
ESTIGATES NATIONAL GE
ATIONAL GEOGRAPHIC
EOGRAPHIC INVESTIGAT
NVESTIGATES NATIONA

Ancient
Celts

Archaeology Unlocks the Secrets of the Celts' Past

Ancient Celts

Archaeology Unlocks the Secrets of the Celts' Past

By Jen Green

Bettina Arnold, Consultant

NATIONAL
GEOGRAPHIC
Washington, DC

Contents

< The ruins of the Celtic fort of Dun Aengus stand on an island off the west coast of
Ireland. Celtic cultural traditions survived longest on the Atlantic fringe of Europe.

◁ Celtic patterns decorate an early Christian cross from Ireland. Irish monks were the first people to write down ancient Celtic myths in the fifth and sixth centuries A.D.

Map of Celtic Peoples

EUROPE

AFRICA

IRELAND

Dun Aengus   Clonycavan
Croghan Bog
Ierne

North Sea
UNITED
KINGDOM

Gundestrup

DENMARK

Lejre

Lindow
Moss   Hasholme

Albion

Verulamium
(St. Albans)   Snettisham
Segsbury Camp
Stonehenge   Camulodunum
(Colchester)
Tintagel   Londinium (London)
Maiden Castle   Butser
Danebury   Hengistbury

*Celtic
Sea*

English Channel

Elbe

GERMANY

Oder

ATLANTIC
OCEAN

Brittany

Seine

Paris

Rhine

Loire   *Gaul*
FRANCE   Vix
Alesia

Hochdorf   Manching

Hallstatt

Danube

Avaricum
(Bourges)   Dijon
Coligny   La Tène

A   L   P   S   AUSTRIA   HUNGARY

SWITZ.

Rhône

*Cisalpine
Gaul*

Galicia

PYRENEES

PORTUGAL   *Tagus*   SPAIN

ITALY

Rome

BA

PENI

GR

Delp

Mediterranean

MOROCCO   ALGERIA

Sea

0   200   400 miles
0   200   400 kilometers

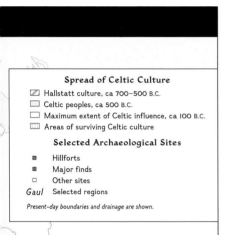

Spread of Celtic Culture

- ▨ Hallstatt culture, ca 700–500 B.C.
- ☐ Celtic peoples, ca 500 B.C.
- ☐ Maximum extent of Celtic influence, ca 100 B.C.
- ▦ Areas of surviving Celtic culture

Selected Archaeological Sites

- ▪ Hillforts
- ▪ Major finds
- ☐ Other sites
- *Gaul*   Selected regions

Present-day boundaries and drainage are shown.

Dnieper

UKRAINE

Black Sea

Galatia

TURKEY ANATOLIA

ASIA MINOR

If your family is from Europe, you can claim Celtic ancestry. The Celtic-speaking peoples of Europe left us lots of clues about their lives, from fortified towns to jewelry, weapons, and beautifully crafted objects. The museums of Europe are filled with what is left of a complex tribal world that once stretched from Spain in the west to the Black Sea in the east.

Why study the Celts? There are many reasons. They left their mark on Europe's landscape from 800 B.C. until the arrival of the Romans and beyond. They brought us iron tools that would remain unchanged until the Industrial Revolution, interlace art still seen today as tattoos on thousands of biceps, a complex musical tradition, and beautiful and strange tales that are a key part of European literature. The Celts were the first Europeans to emerge from the mists of time with faces and voices that still echo in modern traditions like Halloween and the practice of tossing coins into fountains while making a wish. Most of what we know about these people with no writing system of their own is locked in the earth, where archaeologists continue to work to uncover it so their story can be told in books like this one.

Bettina Arnold
Milwaukee, 2007

THREE MAJOR PERIODS OF
Celtic Europe

Hallstatt Period

ca 800—450 B.C.

The first signs of Celtic culture emerged around the eighth century B.C. in an area in what is now Austria, Germany, France, and Switzerland. The culture was named for the site of an Iron Age cemetery found in Austria in the late 19th century: Hallstatt. The Hallstatt period marked the start of iron working in Europe. Hallstatt culture and its characteristic geometric art were found across most of Europe during this time, and there may have been contact with southeastern England as well.

La Tène Period

ca 450—50 B.C.

By 450 B.C. new centers of Celtic power were emerging as armed bands of Celts settled new areas, aided by their iron working skills and their ability as warriors. This period of Celtic culture, named La Tène for an archaeological site in Switzerland, was marked by a new artistic style of swirls and human or animal forms. In artistic terms, La Tène reached its height by about 250 B.C., but the Celtic peoples lacked any equivalent political unity.

< This drinking vessel was made of wood covered with sheets of bronze. The Celts were outstanding metalworkers.

Timeline of Celtic Europe

800

ca 600 B.C. Large hillforts are built in Europe and in southern Britain

ca 400 B.C. Celtic tribes begin to migrate from homelands

400

390 B.C. Celtic warriors sack Rome

279 B.C. Celts sack oracle at Delphi in Greece

50 B.C. Julius Caesar brings Gaul under Roman control

0

A.D. 43 Roman troops invade Britain

A.D. 60 Boudicca leads a revolt in Britain

A.D. 235–285 Romans abandon forts on the Limes; Germanic tribes move across former Celtic lands

400

Romano–Celtic Period

◄ Hallstatt Period 　 La Tène Period

< This sword handle in the shape of a man was found in a grave in Ireland. It was probably made in the first century B.C. Similar handles have been found in Europe.

Romano–Celtic Period

ca 50 B.C. — A.D. 476

The Celts came into increasing conflict with the Roman Empire. In the Gallic Wars of 58–50 B.C., the Romans conquered Gaul and in the first century A.D. much of Britain. Many Celts were assimilated into the Roman Empire. Some Celts were able to preserve their own culture, but often because they lived at the fringes of their former territory, beyond the reach of Rome, as in the case of Ireland. Later migrations of Germanic and Slavic-speaking peoples impacted some areas more than others; Wales and Brittany, for example, maintained their Celtic languages while Germany and eastern Europe did not.

< This gold armband, found in a grave at Hochdorf in Germany, was worn by a nobleman.

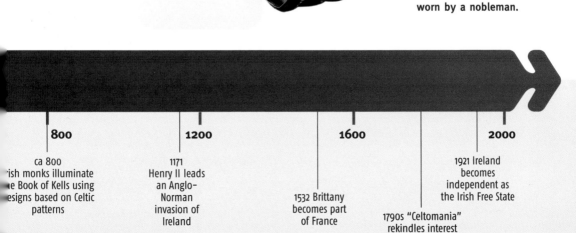

800	1200	1600	2000

ca 800
ish monks illuminate
ie Book of Kells using
esigns based on Celtic
patterns

ic migrants push native Britons
es and other western regions

1171
Henry II leads
an Anglo-
Norman
invasion of
Ireland

1532 Brittany
becomes part
of France

1790s "Celtomania"
rekindles interest
in the Celts
throughout Europe

1921 Ireland
becomes
independent as
the Irish Free State

Yesterday Comes Alive

CHAPTER 1

How do we learn what we know about the past?

Every April 30, thousands of people gather on Carlton Hill in Edinburgh, Scotland. As night falls, a procession climbs the hill. Some people in the parade wear bright costumes; others wear only loincloths. Their blue- or red-painted bodies shine in the light of thousands of flames. Paraders carry flaming torches, jugglers throw burning clubs into the air, and fire-eaters shoot flames from their mouths. Arches burn as symbols of the entrance to the world of the spirits.

Beltain, the fire festival, has been celebrated for over two thousand years. Among the Celtic-speaking

< **A ring of flame seems to surround a costumed performer during Beltain celebrations in Edinburgh.**

Trick or treat!

Halloween might seem an unusual subject for scholars. In fact, it reveals a lot—if you know what you are looking for. The link between Halloween and ghosts, for example, reflects the Celts' belief that the dead could enter the world of the living.

That skeleton costume? Perhaps it started because the Celts made human sacrifices at Samhain. The candy in your trick-or-treat bucket? A modern version of the offerings the living made so that the spirits left them alone.

The experts who put together a picture of how ancient people lived are called archaeologists. They are history's detectives: Sometimes they have very little information to work with, so it is vital to learn as much as possible from every kind of clue, even a Halloween costume.

Tradition or trash?

Popular traditions are a visible part of Celtic culture. They are continued by people who claim descent from the Celts, including the Irish, Welsh, and Scots, the Cornish and Manx of England, the Bretons in France, and the Galicians in Spain. Festivals,

∧ Halloween lanterns have their roots in Celtic celebrations. Ancient peoples hollowed out turnips to make lanterns, which they placed in their windows in order to warn spirits to keep away.

peoples who lived in west-central Europe from about 800 B.C. to A.D. 476, the festival welcomed the light half of the year: summer. Villagers lit bonfires as a form of magic to protect their farm animals from disease and ensure that crops would grow well.

Six months later, the festival of Samhain marked summer's end. The Celts brought animals into shelter, made sacrifices to their gods, and played tricks on one another. Samhain is still important, but it is now known by another name: Halloween.

sports, dances, music, and languages are all often referred to as Celtic.

Archaeologists take such claims with a grain of salt. Often there is no real evidence that links modern and ancient practices. Even though the Celts seem to be one of the most familiar of all ancient peoples, they are also one of the most mysterious. It is often difficult to separate the truth from myths and legends. This is because the Celts did not have a writing system of their own, but passed their traditions down in the form of stories and songs.

Identity crisis

The first challenge is the biggest: Just who were the Celts? The name refers to many groups, rather than one people. These hundreds of tribes had different ways of life and were not related, although many shared similar languages or artistic styles, or a belief in similar gods. In that way, the word *Celt* resembles the phrase Native American: It describes peoples who

▼ **Some of the most remarkable traces of the Celts are bog bodies—human sacrifices who have been preserved for centuries in waterlogged ground.**

Celtic? Says who?

In 1998 British archaeologist Simon James came up with a revolutionary theory. He suggested that modern British and Irish people whom we think of as Celts—and who think of themselves as Celts—may not be descended from Celtic peoples at all.

Most archaeologists believe that Celts from Europe introduced their languages and traditions to Britain and Ireland. But James argues that there is no evidence that large numbers of Celts ever moved to Britain and Ireland. He says that similarities between the peoples of Britain and the Celts—such as their weapons, forts, and jewelry—only show that they had close ties, not that they were related.

James's theory has support from old and new sources. Over two thousand years ago the Romans who left the first written records of the ancient Britons did not call them Celts. They noted how different the Britons were from the peoples of Europe. Red hair was far more common in Britain, for example.

In 2005 David Miles from Oxford University, in England, used the latest research to show that modern Britons are very similar to their ancestors of 12,000 years ago. Miles's evidence was based on analysis of DNA, a chemical code that all living things pass on to their offspring. The code defines the genes that shape the characteristics of the young plant or animal. In humans, DNA is the reason that we inherit characteristics such as eye color or height from our parents.

Scientists took DNA from ancient skeletons and compared it with DNA they gathered from modern Britons. They discovered that people from the Ice Age and modern Britons shared more than 80 percent of the same DNA. Despite the arrival of waves of invaders over the centuries, the genetic nature of the Britons has remained remarkably stable.

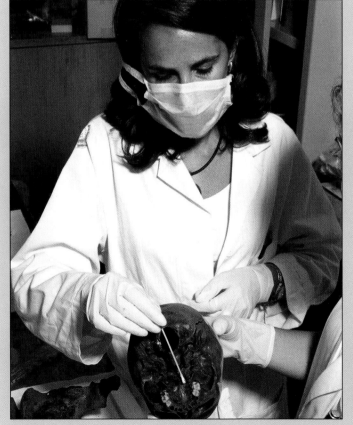

< A scientist extracts DNA from an ancient skull for testing. DNA allows experts to connect living people with their ancestors.

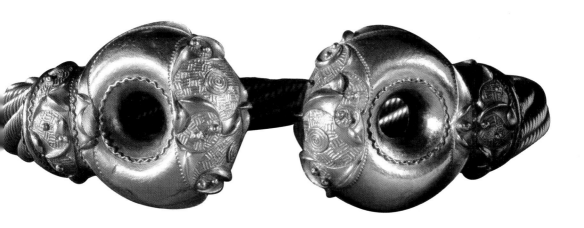

The Snettisham torque was made of threads of gold twisted into ropes which were twined together. The ornament was worn around the throat by elite members of Celtic society.

share a common heritage—but who may be different in important ways. Some experts argue that the term Celt is so vague that it should not be used.

What's in a name?

The name Celt was first used by the ancient Greeks to describe people living in southern France in the fifth century B.C. These people may have called themselves *Keltoi*. Later, the Romans called the same people *Galli*, or Gauls. Today, the term *Celt* is used to refer to peoples found in much of Europe starting in the eighth century B.C. The period is sometimes called the Iron Age, because Europeans started using iron to make tools and weapons. Celtic languages and culture are found from Spain in the west to Turkey in the east during this early period.

Written records

Many popular ideas about the Celts began with Greek and Roman authors. But historians are wary of such accounts. The Celts often clashed

with their neighbors. In 390 B.C., Celtic warriors raided Rome, for example. Rome's response was a military build-up that ultimately helped create the Roman Empire. Perhaps it is no real surprise that classical authors emphasized the Celts' warlike nature.

Witness one: Strabo, a Greek geographer in the first century B.C., noted that the Celts were "madly fond of war." Witness two: Diodorus Siculus, another Greek from the same period, said that the Celts "cut off the heads of their enemies slain in battle."

Witness three: Strabo, again, noted the Celts' "childish boastfulness and love of decoration." Witness four: Ammianus Marcellinus, a Greco-Roman historian of the fourth century A.D.: "The Gauls are all exceedingly careful of cleanliness and neatness."

Witness five: Julius Caesar, the Roman general who conquered Gaul

Celtic calendar

Confirmation that the Celts kept careful track of sesaonal holy dates came in 1897. Along the banks of a stream in northern France farm workers found about 100 pieces of bronze plate engraved with writing. When scholars put them together, they soon realized that they were looking at a calendar. A panel 5 feet wide and 3 feet high (1.5 by 0.9 m) divided a period of 5 years into lunar months, listing and numbering each day. There were holes next to the days so that a wooden peg could mark the date. Although the writing and numbers were Roman, the names of the months and festivals—including Beltain and Samhain—were not in Latin but in a Celtic language. The so-called Coligny Calendar, named for where it was found, dates from around the second century A.D. It records the cycles of the sun and moon highly accurately, and shows that the Celts had mastered the study of astronomy and the measurement of the year.

∧ The Coligny Calendar is one of the longest Celtic inscriptions found so far.

in the first century B.C. said that the Celts were "addicted to religion."

Ancient origins

Warlike headhunters; vain boasters; religious fanatics: The ancient case against the Celts is clear. But how does it compare to the physical evidence? Experts have studied Celtic remains from artifacts made of bronze or iron to huge earthworks and vanished settlements. The evidence they have found confirms ancient accounts—but also gives a broader view.

We'll see in Chapter 5 how Celtic resistance to Rome showed that the Celts were indeed great fighters. Brooches from Iberia (modern Spain

< This head from the Czech Republic dates to the second or first centuries B.C. and probably shows a warrior or a god. The head had great importance for the Celts: They believed it was the home of the soul.

enemies. As Chapter 4 reveals, the Celts were also great traders. Their leaders enjoyed luxury items such as gold jewelry. Such possessions sometimes turn up in Celtic tombs. They suggest that Strabo may have been right that the Celts were great show-offs—but perhaps not because they were vain. In a world of many tribes and chiefs, showing off might have been an important way for people to demonstrate their power and wealth to their neighbors.

Keeping clean for the gods

Chapter 2 reinforces what Marcellinus had to say about good grooming. It tells

V The fingers of a man buried in a bog in Ireland reflect the importance of keeping the nails trimmed and neat. Analysis showed that the man had never done any manual work, and that he was probably a member of an elite class.

and Portugal), for example, have carved images of warriors with heads hanging from their horses. Celtic skulls are also often found without any skeleton, sometimes with holes drilled in them where they were attached to some surface or used in special rituals.

Part of the story

But warfare is only part of the story. As you'll learn in Chapter 3, most Celts were farmers who put more labor into growing crops and raising livestock than they did into fighting their

The Bones of Maiden Castle

When British archaeologist Mortimer Wheeler found more than 50 skeletons at the hillfort of Maiden Castle in southern England in the 1930s, he saw that some of the male skeletons had terrible injuries. Wheeler concluded that they had died defending the fort from the Romans in A.D. 43. Today, archaeologists have other ideas. They point out that only a minority of the dead had such injuries. Most of the bodies were carefully buried, with possessions such as jewelry, pottery, and even joints of meat. It does not

⋀ **Warriors lie in the cemetery at Maiden Castle. One body was found to have a spear tip still lodged between the bones of its spine.**

seem as if they were buried quickly during a fight. Instead, the skeletons may mark a cemetery used over a period of time. The wounded men were likely injured in fighting, but perhaps against their neighbors—and their wounds may not have killed them. The community may have been home to old warriors who bore the scars of their former battles.

the story of 2,000-year-old bodies with perfect fingernails—and hair gel! But again there is another side to the story. The bodies were sacrifices, so the Celts may have linked being clean with being pure and with reverence for the gods.

That brings us to Caesar's claim that the Celts were very religious. Human sacrifice is certainly one sign

that people believe their gods are very powerful. There is more evidence, too. For example, archaeologists have found many swords and daggers on the bed of Lake Neuchâtel at La Tène in Switzerland. Wooden posts in the lake appear to have supported several walkways, which scholars believe once led to a shrine. Pilgrims

may have dropped precious objects into the water from the walkways, for example as offerings to the gods before setting out on a journey. That fit with La Tène's location at a crossroads where Swiss lakes linked with a river network crossing the heart of Europe.

∧ This iron shield boss is decorated with swirling lines typical of art of the late Iron Age or La Tène period. It was found in the Thames River in London, and may have been an offering to the river god.

Holes in the record

Not all questions about the Celts can be answered by archaeology, however. The historical record is full of holes—sometimes actual holes. Archaeologists have to reconstruct whole buildings using only the pattern of holes in the ground that once held wooden posts. Another problem is telling whether physical remains belong to Celts or to, say, Germanic tribes who had a similar way of life. As you'll see in this book, however, careful work is revealing a picture of the Celts that is far more complex than the classical writers' description of "barbarians"— and far more fascinating.

The Bodies in the Bog

Why did the Celts make human sacrifices?

Something was wrong. From the cab of his digger, Larry Corley could see a solid object sticking out of the ditch he was clearing at the edge of the Croghan bog in County Offaly in northeastern Ireland in May 2003. When he jumped down for a closer look, Corley was shocked to see that the object was a human arm ending in a large hand. He called the Gardaí, the Irish police, and covered the arm to protect it. A policeman soon

< This Celtic body found in Germany was thought to be female. Later tests showed that the victim was a boy; his "blindfold" is a hair band that slipped over his eyes.

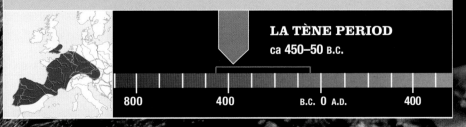

LA TÈNE PERIOD
ca 450–50 B.C.

800   400   B.C. 0 A.D.   400

Examining the Bog Bodies

Archaeologists analyzing the remains of bog bodies use cutting-edge techniques in their investigations. A procedure called electron spin resonance, for example, allows experts to trace when an object has been heated or cooled, and how much. Analysis of the contents of a body found in England showed that he had eaten bread shortly before his death. The bread had been baked at such a high heat that parts of it were burned—perhaps deliberately. Celtic legends tell how victims were chosen for sacrifice after choosing a piece of burned bread in a kind of lottery. The man's stomach also held mistletoe, which Roman writers said the Celts used in ceremonies, including ritual sacrifice.

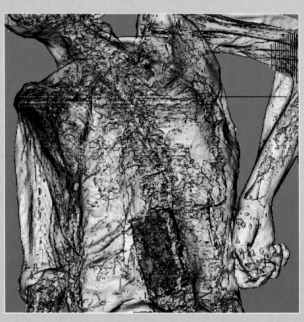

∧ X-rays reveal bones inside bog bodies, as in this false-color image of Graubølle Man from Denmark. The brown area shows where ribs were removed for analysis.

arrived with a pathologist, expecting to find the victim of a modern murder. Peat bogs were a common place to find people killed in the terrorist conflict in nearby Northern Ireland in the 1970s and 1980s. But when the men pulled back the black plastic, the pathologist realized that this victim was much older. The body was well preserved—and later tests showed that it was about 2,200 years old.

Ancient murder mystery

The investigation passed to experts from the National Museum of Ireland. They dug up the body, leaving wet peat around it to preserve it, and took it to the museum in Dublin. The body, which was named Old Croghan Man for the ditch where it was found, was actually a torso. But it still provided a huge amount of information.

The man was in his 20s when he died—and he was indeed the victim of a murder. There are holes in his upper arms through which a rope was threaded to tie his arms behind his body. Cuts on his body suggest that he was tortured before he was beheaded, cut in half, and thrown into the bog. The man was naked, apart from a leather band tied around his left arm.

Surprises from the peat

From his arm span, experts figured out that the man was very tall: About six feet six inches (198 cm). That was a surprise: Other bodies suggest that ancient people tended to be somewhat smaller than modern humans.

Another surprise lay at the end of the arms. The fingernails had been polished and manicured. Experts used an electron microscope to examine the nails. The microscope fires beams of particles at objects to create far more detailed images than a light-based microscope. The images confirmed that the nails were those of someone who did no manual labor. The man had probably held a very high position in society.

Analysis showed that the nails contained a high level of nitrogen. The chemical is created in the body by eating high-protein foods, such as meat and fish. That suggested the

man had died in the winter, when there were few vegetables to eat. The contents of his stomach showed that his final meal had been some wheat and buttermilk.

To the archaeologists, it seemed

∧ Old Croghan Man's torso was soaked in liquid paraffin and then freeze-dried to preserve it.

∨ Bogs are formed when waterlogged areas become home to moss and other plants, which decompose to form peat. Without oxygen, organic material, such as bodies, is protected from bacteria that cause decay.

that the tall, strong, young man had come from the elite of society. He had been murdered in a ritual that seemed to be connected with a sacrifice. It might even be that the man had gone willingly to his death.

The long and the short

Old Croghan Man was not alone. At least 2,000 bodies have been found in bogs in northern Europe. Many had died in similar rituals. Only three months before the body was found at Croghan bog, the team from the National Museum of Ireland had learned about another body, Clonycavan Man, found only 25 miles (40 km) away. This time the victim had been short—five foot two inches (158 cm). But archaeologists believe that he tried to make up for his lack of height in a remarkable way: He piled up his hair on top of his head. To hold it in place, he used an early form of hair gel.

Beauty secrets

Stephen Buckley, from the University of York in England, found that the hair gel was made by mixing vegetable oil with resin, a sticky substance produced by trees. But when Buckley analyzed the resin, he found that it did not come from Ireland. He traced it to pine trees that grew in Spain and southwestern France. The resin must have come to Ireland through trade. That would mean it was expensive—and that Clonycavan Man was another member of the elite.

The two Irish bog bodies surprised most archaeologists Celtic sacrifice was well known, but experts had thought that the victims

< Clonycavan Man was found with his face pushed into his chest, but archaeologists have been able to move the head back to make the face visible.

<A photographer uses a computer to help take a picture of a bog body.

probably came from the lower classes of society or were people who had broken the rules of the community, as Classical authors like Caesar suggest. If the sacrifices were aristocrats, that would mean the explanation might be more complex.

Bodies and boundaries

Ned Kelly, keeper of antiquities at the National Museum of Ireland, compared the location of 40 bodies found in Irish bogs. He realized that they all occurred along ancient boundaries between tribes. The same boundaries were marked by artifact deposits in bogs, such as weapons, jewelry, and golden crowns and collars.

Kelly knew that such objects were often associated with Celtic kings. Perhaps both the objects and the bodies had been placed in the bogs by kings as offerings to make the tribe's land inside the boundary more fertile.

∧ The toes of a detached foot, found at Südmentzhausen in Germany, peek from a legging that was fashionable in the Roman period.

Warring peoples

Kelly suggests that the sacrifices may have been high-status hostages from other tribes. They may have been nobles captured in warfare or raids. Experts are still considering whether the theory holds up—but it is a reminder that the Celts were not a single people. Tribes traded with one another or cooperated in times of war. But an individual's loyalty was to his or her tribe—to die for it, or to kill for it.

Widespread Way of Life

CHAPTER 3

What do we know about how the Celts lived?

Silversmiths make patterns in a piece of metal by using hammers and small tools called punches to tap out a design. Every tap is different. Perhaps the smith holds the hammer in a certain way, or perhaps a punch has a rough edge that leaves an uneven mark. The punch marks bear the unique signature of the tool that made them, like the keys of a typewriter, each with its own microscopic flaws. Using a powerful microscope, an expert can identify which tool made which marks,

< The base of the Gundestrup Cauldron has a carving called the Dying Bull. Some experts believe the image is linked to Celtic myth, but no one knows for sure.

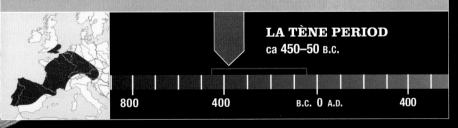

LA TÈNE PERIOD
ca 450–50 B.C.

800   400   B.C. 0 A.D.   400

and possibly whether different pieces were made in the same workshop. That is how archaeologists in the 1980s learned that the Gundestrup Cauldron, a silver vessel found in Denmark a century earlier, was produced using five different tools.

Meet the Smiths

Discovering that the cauldron had as many as five possible makers was a remarkable piece of detective work—but it only solved half the mystery. We know there were several smiths, but archaeologists do not agree on where the cauldron was actually made.

They do know some facts, however. Fact: The cauldron is 27 inches (69 cm) across, is 97 percent pure silver, and weighs nearly 20 pounds (9 kg).

∧ No one knows where the Gundestrup Cauldron was made. The style and technique of the silverwork resembles work produced by the Scordisci, Celts from Thrace, a region in modern Greece and Turkey.

Fact: It was made in the late second or first century B.C. Fact: Its reliefs show Celtic themes. Fact: It is so big that it was probably used in religious rituals. Fact: It was probably placed in a bog or swamp as an offering to the gods. But that's where the facts run out and the questions begin.

Where was the vessel made? Some experts identify figures on it as gods worshiped by Celts in northern Gaul. That would mean it came from modern-day France. Other scholars disagree. They point out that the punched dots and crisscross lines that represent the fur of animals were

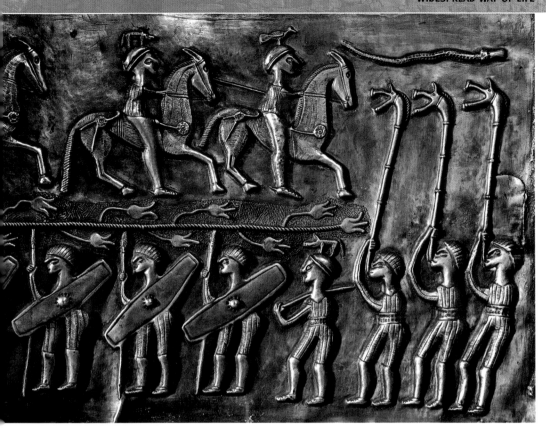

used by metalworkers from much farther away: Thrace, in the Balkans of southeast Europe. Smiths there had been influenced by metalworking styles from Persia to the east.

Tracing a route

But what would a Thracian treasure be doing in a bog thousands of miles to the north? There are a number of theories. One is that the cauldron crossed Europe as the result of trade. Another is that it was seized as booty by Danish warriors, perhaps in the Roman army. Another is that the cauldron was commissioned from Thracian smiths—by a Celtic tribe named the Scordisci, who had settled in Thrace. Perhaps the cauldron was seized from the Scordisci by the

∧ This panel from the Gundestrup Cauldron shows a Celtic army: Trumpeters (*right*), cavalry (*top*), and foot soldiers (*bottom left*).

∨ The god Cernunnos appears in another panel. His horns link him with stags, symbols of fertility.

801234567

Pollen analysis

Information about Celtic farming comes not only from iron tools but also from pollen. These tiny grains, which plants use to reproduce, have a tough outer casing, so they last for much longer than leafy or woody parts of plants. Pollen is therefore a great way to learn what plants once grew in an area. When experts find pollen from trees such as oaks dominating the soil layer during the Celtic era, they know that forests covered the landscape. The pollen of crops and other light-loving plants shows that the land had been cleared for farming. By the end of the Hallstatt period, pollen records suggest that many parts of Europe were under cultivation.

▼ **Electron micrograph image of pollen from species that grew in Iron Age Europe: dandelion (yellow and green) and horse chestnut (brown)**

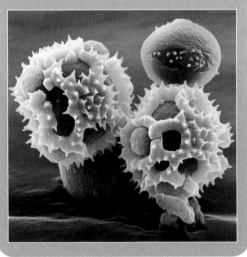

Cimbri, a Germanic people who attacked their lands in 120 B.C. and could have carried the cauldron north.

The solution to the mystery may lie at a microscopic level. It should be possible to compare the "signatures" of the Gundestrup Cauldron smiths to other silverwork. If experts find a match on another object, that could help identify where the smiths lived. But it's a big job. The punch marks are far smaller than needles—and the haystack might be the size of Europe.

The Celts spread

The journey of the Gundestrup cauldron is just one sign of the extent of the Celtic world. By about 250 B.C., Celts had settled regions from Portugal to Ukraine. Most were farmers. They used iron tools to clear land to grow crops. Analysis of pollen, the dustlike material plants use to reproduce, shows that many wooded areas were cleared, either to make space for farmland or to provide wood to use in mines or furnaces.

Across Europe, archaeologists have found traces of Celtic settlements. Often they are marked by little more than holes in the ground. The holes once supported the wooden poles of houses, granaries, and other buildings, but the wood has rotted away. It is not easy to tell which hole belonged to which building. Danebury Hillfort in southern England, for example, has 18,000 postholes. Reconstructing the pattern of its buildings is like doing a huge dot-to-dot puzzle.

Celtic homes

Celtic homes in Britain and the Iberian Peninsula were roundhouses 20 to 30 feet (6–9 m) across. In other parts of the continent, homes were

rectangular and often quite large, with many rooms. The pattern of postholes shows how the houses were built, with beams sloping in from an outer circle to join at the top or with a long central roof beam. The walls were made of willow branches woven together and smeared with a paste of mud and animal manure, although stone was used in areas of Ireland or Spain where wood was scarce. No one knows for sure what the Celts used to roof their homes. They probably made thatch from bundles of reeds.

Storage specialists

Archaeologists excavating Danebury in the 1970s and 1980s found the

∧ The hillfort at Danebury in southern Britain was home to a settlement for about 500 years. Postholes show that a larger building stood at the center of the settlement: It may have been a shrine or temple.

remains of spelt wheat and barley, which were the main grains in the Celts' diet. Storing grain through the winter was vital. Danebury had granaries with raised floors to keep out dampness and rats. Grain was stored in pottery jars or wooden bins for daily use. But there were also five thousand bell-shaped pits dug into the ground. They were filled with grain and the narrow openings sealed with clay so that they were airtight.

Archaeologists at Butser Ancient Farm Research Center in southern

Back to the Iron Age

< An outhouse at Butser shows the basic Celtic building technique in Britain: A conical roof of thatch rises above a low, round wall of wattle and daub, a framework of saplings coated in dried mud.

∨ The inside of a house at Butser shows the raw timber frame of the building. The open fireplace was used for cooking and heating in the cold British winters.

One method archaeologists use to explore how the Celts lived is to reconstruct Iron Age settlements. Experts use a combination of physical evidence and written accounts—and common sense—to build villages as the Celts did. In the 1970s, Danish archaeologist Hans-Ole Hansen built a Celtic village at Lejre. Every summer, families live as Celts there. Another reconstruction was built at Butser in southern England by Peter Reynolds. Reynolds used tools based on Iron Age originals to grow crops the Celts had grown. Local farmers agreed not to use fertilizers nearby, so that the crops would grow entirely as they had in ancient times. Not all such experiments have been successful. When the British Broadcasting Corporation (BBC) re-created an Iron Age settlement for a reality TV show in 2001, many contestants got sick from poor food and hygiene, and were exhausted by the hard farming lifestyle.

England re-created similar pits in the 1980s. They filled each with a ton of wheat, and used sensors to measure changes in the gas in the pit. When the pits were opened a year later, the sensors told the story. As grains at the top or sides of the pit sprouted, they used up oxygen and gave off carbon dioxide. Carbon dioxide killed germs that might make the grain rot. The result? Only two percent of the grain was spoiled. The rest was perfect to grind into flour for bread or to plant to produce a new crop.

You're such a boar!

The Celts also raised animals. A team studying Segsbury Camp in southern England analyzed more than 1,500 pieces of animal bone and teeth. They found that sheep were the most common animal, but that cows were more important for food, because each cow yielded more meat than each sheep. The bones show that the animals were usually killed when they were young. That suggests that they were more valued for their meat than for their wool or their milk.

Only a few bones at Segsbury came from pigs, but pork was popular at feasts. Many Celts believed that the wild pig, or boar, was sacred. In Galicia, archaeologists have found small tablets of bronze shaped like wild boars and covered in Latin script. These are called *tesserae hospitalis*, or tablets of hospitality. The documents recorded pacts between individuals or communities to offer one another friendship. The pacts formed links between people from different settlements. Experts think that the pacts were almost as important as families or tribes in organizing society.

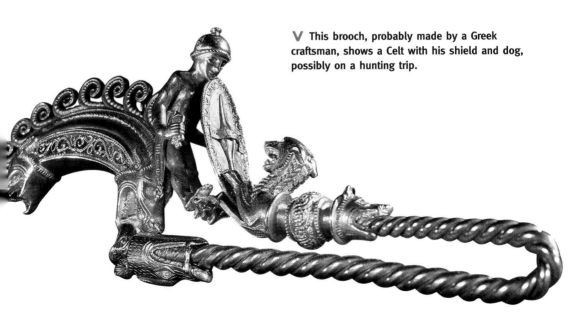

∨ **This brooch, probably made by a Greek craftsman, shows a Celt with his shield and dog, possibly on a hunting trip.**

Iron, Trade, and Water

CHAPTER 4

How did the Celts become great traders?

German archaeologist Jörg Biel was disappointed. Part of his job at the state department of antiquities was to follow up tips from local residents about possible ancient sites. In spring 1978, schoolteacher Renate Liebfried had called from the small village of Hochdorf, near Stuttgart. She invited him to inspect several mounds that might hold ancient tombs, but when Biel got to Hochdorf he found nothing very interesting. Then, as

< Archaeologists carefully study one of the many 2,500-year-old artifacts discovered in the tomb at Hochdorf.

HALLSTATT PERIOD ca 800–450 B.C.
LA TÈNE PERIOD ca 450–50 B.C.

800   400   B.C. 0 A.D.   400

he turned to go, the schoolteacher drew his attention to the remains of a mound that lay northeast of the village. This time Biel was excited. Similar mounds had often contained the tombs of Iron Age chieftains—and the Hochdorf mound was huge.

A chieftain's burial

For months, Biel's team dug into the mound. As they worked, they found objects such as jewelry that suggested not only that this was a tomb, but also that it was intact. It had not been raided by treasure-seekers. Eventually, at the heart of the mound, Biel uncovered what he called the "find of a lifetime." In a chamber the remains of a tall Celtic chieftain lay on a bronze couch supported by female statuettes.

The Hochdorf chief had been laid to rest with a gold torque or necklace around his neck, a dagger with a hilt covered in sheet gold by his side, and gold strips on his shoes. Scattered around the warrior were possessions including a wagon and a fine robe. There was also a great bronze cauldron, to mix and serve alcohol. Chemical analysis of its contents showed that the chieftain had been buried with 92 gallons (350 l) of a honey-based drink called mead.

The Hochdorf tomb is one of the richest of a number of Celtic tombs dating from around the sixth century B.C. The luxury objects they contain

▽ **Based on archaeologists' records, this painting re-creates the Hochdorf tomb. The dead chieftain lies on a couch beside a wagon loaded with bronze.**

show how wealthy Celtic rulers had become. For Biel, the chief's robe was particularly revealing. Analysis showed that it was decorated with embroidery of silk thread—from China! That was evidence that 2,500 years ago the Celts had trade links that stretched not only across Europe but east across Asia.

Wealth from salt

How had the Celts grown so powerful? Part of the answer lies to the southeast in the heart of the Salzburg Mountains in Austria: salt, which the Celts called *hall*. Workers from the town of Hallstatt have been mining rock salt from the Salzburg area for 4,000 years.

Salt was valuable. It was used to stop food from rotting and also as a medicine. Stone Age miners dug tunnels into the mountain, working by the light of pine torches. Archaeologist Fritz Eckart Barth has found the remains of the picks and wooden buckets they used. The salt in the mine has also preserved their leather knapsacks, mittens, and caps.

∧ A restorer carefully cleans part of an iron wheel from the wagon found in the Hochdorf tomb. Each cleaned piece is then added to the plastic frame of the reconstructed wheel.

A Celtic cemetery

Salt from the Salzburg area continued to be mined through to modern times. It was during construction work at the mine in the 19th century that the

∨ This bronze lion decorated a cauldron from Hochdorf. It may have been made in Greece or Italy.

An archaeological pioneer

The Celtic settlement at Hallstatt was found in 1846 by mine director Georg Ramsauer, during the construction of a new road to the mine. Ramsauer uncovered seven graves before winter forced him to stop digging. He resumed excavations in the spring—and continued for the next 17 years. In all, he uncovered a cemetery of nearly 1,000 graves. Unlike many archaeologists of the time,

Ramsauer worked carefully, making detailed notes and drawings of everything he found. Today more than 2,000 graves have been discovered at Hallstatt—but Ramsauer's records remain vital to understanding the secrets of the cemetery.

▽ **Ramsauer found 980 graves at Hallstatt—and made careful records like this watercolor of the contents of every one of them.**

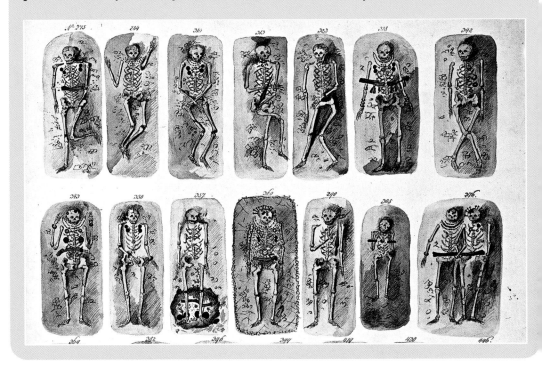

remains were discovered of a huge Celtic cemetery that included more than 2,000 graves.

The dead of Hallstatt were not nobles like the Hochdorf chieftain. But they were still buried with ornaments, tools, and weapons for the afterlife. Experts have found many objects in the graves that were acquired through trade with distant lands: Amber beads from the Baltic, ivory from Africa,

armor from Slovenia, and bronze vessels from Greece and Italy.

The Hallstatt finds were so important that archaeologists gave the name of the site to the first great age of the Celts, from about 800 to 450 B.C. Many objects from the graves were decorated with simple geometric patterns. Archaeologists now identify this angular style as a hallmark of the early Celtic period—the Hallstatt era.

Iron arrives

The objects from the graves confirmed much of what archaeologists already knew. At the start of the Hallstatt era, an important change swept the Celtic world. Earlier peoples had made bronze by heating a mixture of copper and tin. After about 800 B.C., bronze weapons and tools were replaced by iron. The Celts had learned how to heat lumps of iron ore, which is found at many sites in Europe, to extract iron. The new metal was harder than bronze, and easier to work into different shapes. The Celts had not yet mastered how to cast molten iron in molds, however; they still used bronze to make more detailed objects.

Iron-working transformed the Celtic world. Iron tools worked better than ones made of bronze. Iron sickles and hoes—and later plows—made farming more efficient. Using iron axes, the Celts felled forests to bring more land under cultivation and to use as building material and as fuel.

Let's experiment!

Experts often use a relatively new technique to learn about the Celts: experimental archaeology. The name describes a process of trial and error where archaeologists try to re-create how the Celts did things like fire pots in a kiln, for example, or use a furnace to produce iron from iron ore. The starting points for the experiments are contemporary accounts or artifacts, but the experts also gather input from other sources. They may study how peoples today build kilns or furnaces, for example. They may take advice from expert engineers. Or they may simply use their common sense to work out why a process has failed—and try again!

Large areas of Europe were deforested around this time.

Celts in canoes

Iron also enabled the Celts to prosper as traders. By the seventh century B.C., they traded iron goods along with minerals such as salt, copper, and tin.

∨ Bronze and iron meet: An iron Celtic dagger from Hallstatt with a bronze handle and scabbard.

The vessel from Vix

In winter 1953, French archaeologist René Joffroy excavated the Vix mound by the Seine near the hillfort of Mont Lassois. Rain soaked the ground and made digging difficult, but Joffroy found the tomb of a Celtic princess who had died in about 500 B.C. It was the richest burial ever found from the early Iron Age.

The tomb was full of objects associated with power, including a huge bronze vessel used to mix drinks. This krater was remarkable for its size—at 5 feet (1.5 m) tall, it is one of the largest drinking vessels ever made—and for its origin. Lettering and images on the rim show that it was made in Greece.

Joffroy believed that Mont Lassois had grown wealthy because it controlled trade routes. Mont Lassois, he argued, marked the point where British tin carried up the Seine by boat was unloaded to continue its journey south.

∧ The Vix krater is so big that it was probably made in sections and put together afterward.

The boats that carried cargoes along rivers such as the Rhine, Rhône, and Seine varied from hollowed-out logs to more complex vessels. Archaeologists discovered one logboat during drainage work at Hasholme, in northern England, in 1984. It dated from about 300 B.C., when it had sailed on the Humber River. It was carved from a single log 46 feet (14 m) long, with planks added to make the sides deeper. Experts calculate that the boat could carry a crew of five, along with a cargo of 5.5 tons. When it sank, it was carrying timber and joints of meat.

Larger boats have been found in lakes in Switzerland, where the frames of their hulls are preserved on the lakebeds. Sailboats made from planks were used to sail on lakes, rivers, and around Europe's coastlines. The joints between the planks were made waterproof—or caulked—by being stuffed with moss. Fishers in some parts of Europe still use the same means to waterproof their boats.

A coastal port

In the early 1980s, Barry Cunliffe explored Hengistbury Head, a coastal site in southern England. He found evidence of a harbor built where a beach provided mooring for boats. Cunliffe believes that goods arrived

> Archaeologists in Denmark in the early 2000s attempt to create a Celtic log canoe using the same tools the Celts would have used.

by sea and were loaded on to boats to sail inland up rivers. They included jugs from Italy, pottery from France, and figs from the Mediterranean. Exports traveling in the other direction included iron, copper, and lead, corn, and salt.

A sacred element

The Celts saw water as more than a way of transportation. They worshiped nature spirits, including spirits who lived in rivers and springs. French archaeologists exploring a spring near Dijon at the head of the Seine River found carved human figures and body parts—eyes, legs, and kidneys. They believe the offerings were thrown into the water to ask the goddess of the river to heal illness or injury.

In the Thames River in England, meanwhile, the discovery of human bones in 2000 shed light on an old mystery. Not many Celtic burials have been found in Britain or the Iberian Peninsula. On the continent, too, they disappear by the end of the La Tène period. The English team found evidence that funerals had been carried out on sand islands in the river. Perhaps, they suggested, Iron Age people disposed of their dead by burying them in water. That would explain the lack of graves—and underline the importance of rivers, bogs, and lakes in the Celtic world. Cremation—burning—or exposure are other possible ways the Celts may have disposed of the dead.

> This gold model boat was found in Ireland, and may have been an offering. Celtic vessels were 100 feet (30 m) long, and equipped with sails and oars.

The Roman Conquest

CHAPTER 5

What happened when the Romans came?

Colonel Eugène Stoffel had been an officer in the French army. He knew a good defensive spot when he saw one—and now, in 1860, he was looking at one. Stoffel was exploring Mont Auxois near Dijon in Burgundy, France. The rocky crag, rising above a plateau that was once covered in forest, was a fine location for a hillfort. That was just what Stoffel was looking for. The emperor of France, Napoleon III, had asked him to find Alesia, the site of the last stand of the Gauls

⟨ The ramparts of Maiden Castle rise above farmland in southern England. Like Alesia, the hillfort proved unable to hold out against the Roman armies.

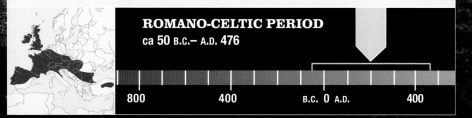

ROMANO-CELTIC PERIOD
ca 50 B.C.– A.D. 476

800   400   B.C. 0 A.D.   400

45

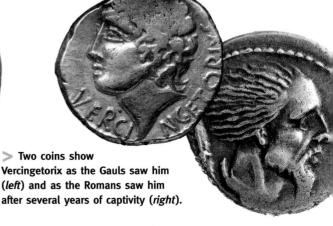

A statue of a Celtic warrior from the Glauberg in Germany dated to the fifth century B.C. The statue's "Mickey Mouse" ears were probably a sign that the individual was an ancestral figure to be worshiped, similar to the halo of a Christian saint.

against Julius Caesar in 52 B.C. The emperor wanted Alesia to be a symbol of French resistance to foreign rule.

Stoffel had a great guide: Caesar himself described his campaigns in *On the Gallic Wars*. But could his account be trusted? He wanted to show himself in a good light because he had political ambitions—and he was successful. In 46 B.C., he became ruler of Rome. Caesar stressed the Gauls' military strength—and his own success in defeating them. In fact, we now know that the Gallic tribes were weak mainly because they were not united.

Working for the emperor brought many advantages, so Stoffel had more than 300 assistants to hunt for clues. They found traces of holes that once supported wooden walls. Holes dotted in front of the walls had held logs set at an angle and sharpened to a point

> Two coins show Vercingetorix as the Gauls saw him (*left*) and as the Romans saw him after several years of captivity (*right*).

Holding out against Rome

The Roman conquest of Gaul is the backdrop for the comic series *Astérix the Gaul*, which was created in Belgium. The strip features a village that holds out after the Roman occupation. Astérix and his buddy Obelix have now taken on the Romans in 33 books. The village inhabitants are based on Celtic stereotypes, such as Cacofonix the minstrel and Vitalstitistix the chief.

Of course, Asterix is only a comic—or is it? In 2007 archaeologists working in Normandy in northwest France discovered a grave from the third century A.D. in which human bones were buried with horse bones. That practice was sometimes carried out by Celts who worshiped Epona, goddess of horses and warriors. But by then Gaul had been under Roman control for 300 years. The experts can't help wondering if, perhaps, one real life village might have clung to its Celtic traditions—just like the village in the comic strip.

< Astérix and Obelix draw the strength to fight the Romans from a secret potion brewed by Getafix, their village Druid.

to slow down enemy forces. But it was only when Stoffel found a hoard of coins that he could be sure he had found Alesia. They bore the name of the legendary leader of the Gallic forces: Vercingetorix.

Partners and enemies

A recent aerial survey used infrared technology to study Alesia. Where soil has been disturbed in the past, such as by construction work, plant life has also been disturbed. It gives off a slightly different amount of heat from nearby vegetation. An infrared image turns tiny changes in temperature into different colors in a scan. That can help show up buried features.

At Alesia, the infrared scans showed the defenses identified by

Stoffel over a century earlier. A ring of deep ditches and high ramparts stretched 9.5 miles (15 km) around the town. The Romans built them to keep 50,000 Gallic warriors trapped inside Alesia—and built a larger ring of defenses to protect themselves from the Celts' allies. After a siege lasting six weeks, Vercingetorix surrendered to save his people: He was executed in Rome a few years later. The Romans had conquered Gaul.

Resistance in Britain

In the following century, the Romans invaded the British Isles. Their troops overcame the great earthworks such as Maiden Castle and took control of southern and eastern Britain. As in France, some leaders tried to resist. The Roman writer Tacitus told how in A.D. 60 the warrior-queen Boudicca led a people named the Iceni south from their homeland in what is now Norfolk. She attacked and burned the Romanized towns of Camulodunum (now Colchester), Verulamium (St. Albans), and Londinium (London), before being defeated by the Romans.

Conflicting evidence

Boudicca remains a popular figure in British mythology. But how accurate is Tacitus? Some archaeologists wonder if he exaggerated details of the revolt to make his story more thrilling for his readers in Rome. At Verulamium and Londinium, they point out, there is little evidence that the settlements were destroyed. Even at Camulodunum, which was burned down, there are no bodies or valuable possessions in the ruins of the town. The inhabitants seem to have had time to clear out before the Iceni burned the town. That's hardly a sign of a ferocious attack.

On the other hand, excavations in

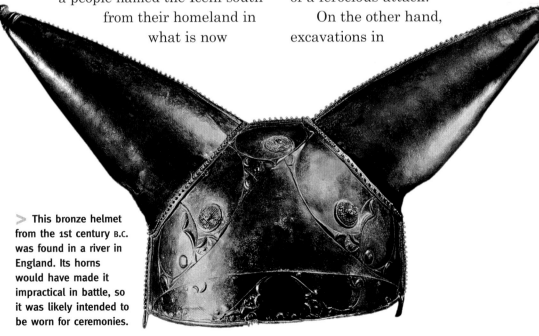

> This bronze helmet from the 1st century B.C. was found in a river in England. Its horns would have made it impractical in battle, so it was likely intended to be worn for ceremonies.

London in 2003 found bodies that seemed to have been buried but dug up soon after and mutilated. A coin found with the bodies dated the event to sometime shortly before A.D. 70. Some archaeologists believe that the desecration must have been carried out by Boudicca's warriors as they rampaged through the town.

A continuing quest

More evidence is needed to reveal the true scale of the revolt. Archaeologists are eager to find either the site of Boudicca's final defeat by the Romans or her grave. But the location of both sites is a mystery. Different experts have suggested that the battle may have taken place anywhere from

Boudicca and her daughters ride in a war chariot in this statue that stands near the Thames River in London. Contemporaries recorded that the tall, red-haired queen was a terrifying sight as she led her warriors into battle.

London to north Wales. As for the grave, one rumor used to say that Boudicca was buried at Stonehenge. No one still believes that is likely. Another popular story says that the warrior-queen is buried beneath Platform 8 at King's Cross railroad station in London. Most serious archaeologists dismiss that, too. They believe that there is as much chance of the story being true as there is of joining Harry Potter to catch the train to Hogwarts from Platform 9 ¾ next door.

Meet an Archaeologist

Susanne Sievers of the German Archaeological Institute has studied several famous Celtic sites like Alesia, the Heuneburg, and Manching. She is a specialist in Celtic settlements and armament.

What made you want to be an archaeologist?
When I was a child, I had a dream: sitting all alone in a wide foreign landscape in fresh air, digging, thinking about forgotten people and waiting for exciting news.

What's the best part of your job?
To be outside and active, to learn new information from excavations or to get impressions from the topography of a landscape. I also like the moments in my office when I have time to write an article or a book.

What's the worst part of your job?
There are parts of my job that have nothing to do with archaeology, such as discussions about money. I have done too much editing work on academic papers, so I don't enjoy it anymore. There are also too many frustrating discussions with colleagues and committee meetings.

What are the most important qualities for an archaeologist?
Curiosity, patience, logical thinking, precision, speaking many languages, imagination.

Is there much left to learn about the ancient Celts?
Every generation of archaeologists asks new questions and gets new answers not only by studying new material, but also by looking again at material that is already well known. In the last few years, we have learned a lot through both new excavations of burial mounds and settlements and through reinterpretation of earlier work. It is important to work with new methods from the natural sciences and new archaeological methods, and it is always stimulating to study other cultures in order to be able to compare them with the ancient Celts. So our picture of the Celts is always changing, even without the new excavations.

What was the most important discovery you've ever made?

A During excavations I usually clean metal objects in the evening and make first descriptions. Once, I cleaned a burned piece of bronze and iron and suddenly there was an eye and minutes later one half of a human face. It was a Celtic face (the head of a linch-pin), looking at me in a very intense way.

Q Do you have any advice for young people who want to become archaeologists?
A You should be good at sports, because excavations can be very hard. You should read about archaeology, and visit museums and sites. You should try to design everyday objects and to describe them. And you should visit foreign countries, if possible.

Q What techniques have been most useful for your work at Manching?
A The fortified settlement (*oppidum*) of Manching measures 1.5 square miles (380 ha). That's a lot. Much has already been destroyed, for instance by a small airport. But the pilots help us by taking photos from the air. We are also using methods like georadar or geophysics to study what is underneath the surface. From the wooden houses only postholes, ditches, or pits are left, filled with rubbish and earth. So in the end our eyes are our most important instruments to

∧ An aerial view of the oppidum at Manching, where Susanne Sievers is one of the directors of excavations.

detect differences in the color of the earth and to be able to interpret what we see.

Q Can we learn about the Celts through experimental archaeology?
A Yes and no. We can learn something about the techniques they used, like making pottery, weaving, forging. We can see that their wool clothes were scratchy to wear. But we can't learn how the Celts were thinking, feeling, dreaming, believing, or what made them happy or anxious.

Q How were the Romans able to defeat the Gauls relatively easily?
A In my opinion it wasn't

easy. When I was excavating at Alesia, where Caesar fought the Gauls, I saw the Roman lines and the effort it took the Romans to besiege the oppidum and also to be aware of the army coming together from the whole country to liberate the besieged Gauls. Caesar spent seven years in what we now call France before he came to this point. The Roman army was better organized and the Gauls were quarreling all the time; some were even confederates of the Romans. And the Romans were allied with the Germans. So, there are many factors which are responsible for this victory.

A Living Legacy

CHAPTER 6

What happened to Celtic culture?

Rosalind Niblett knows more about the Roman town of Verulamium than anyone else. It's not surprising. She grew up nearby and, after she trained as an archaeologist, spent fifty years exploring the site in modern St. Albans. In the 1990s she found the tomb of a British chieftain who was buried with Roman luxury goods, including a dinner service. After the Roman conquest, it was clear that some Britons cooperated with their new rulers. Near the tomb lay another fascinating discovery: The remains of a temple built around A.D. 90. Niblett found artifacts inside the temple that she believes show that it was

< On Midsummer Day, June 21, Druids welcome the sunrise at Stonehenge. They believe they are enacting an ancient ritual—but the experts are not so sure.

Barbarians or heroes?

With virtually no written language of their own, much of what we know about Celtic culture comes from Greek and Roman writings. However these accounts are often hostile. Greek and Roman writers regularly described the Celts as barbarians and said that they were often drunk. The Greek historian Diodorus Siculus was horrified by Celtic table manners: "When they are eating, the moustache becomes entangled in the food, and when they are drinking, the drink passes, as it were, through a sort of strainer."

But the Romans did admire Celtic bravery. The Gallic warrior became a kind of ideal for other ancient peoples, as shown by the statue called "The Dying Gaul," made in a Greek colony in Turkey around the third century B.C.

◁ **"The Dying Gaul" shows a wounded warrior wearing a torque, his sword lying by his side.**

in use for at least two hundred years—and that Celtic gods were worshiped there alongside the gods of Britain's new Roman rulers.

Elsewhere, too, elements of Celtic culture survived, especially on the edges of Europe that did not come under Roman rule. In the so-called Celtic Fringe—Ireland, Scotland, Wales, Brittany in France, and the northwestern corner of Spain—many people today claim descent from the Celts and fiercely defend their culture.

The Druids

Other people also find Celtic heritage attractive. They include Neopagans who follow a religion they say is based on ancient beliefs, including those of the Celts. Roman writers reported that the Celts used priests called Druids to communicate with the gods and carry out human sacrifices. While the Romans ended such practices in most of Gaul and England, it was only the arrival of Christianity centuries later that ended pagan worship in other parts of the Celtic world.

The Druids have not completely vanished. Every year on Midsummer Day, hundreds of Druids greet the dawn at Stonehenge in southwest England. They believe that the ritual has ancient roots. Experts point out that Stonehenge was built about 4,000 years ago—long before Celts

lived in Britain. Today's Druids, they argue, say more about modern people and what they want to believe than they do about the ancient world.

New influences

Between A.D. 250 and 500, new waves of settlers displaced Celts throughout Europe. The Franks took control of northern France while Alemannian tribes occupied southwest Germany, Slavs took over eastern Europe, and Visigoths ruled in Spain.

Angles and Saxons from northern Germany and Denmark settled in Britain, bringing a new culture and a new language, which became English. In 1066 England was conquered by Normans from France. For centuries, English rulers fought to impose control in Celtic-speaking Scotland, Ireland, and Wales. But they never succeeded in entirely wiping out the people who lived there or their culture.

△ **This drawing from the early 1800s shows Druids dancing around Stonehenge—but it was only based on guesswork. In fact, Druids are highly unlikely to have carried out rituals at the site.**

Keeping Celtic

In the fifth century, missionaries had spread Christianity to Ireland, where it replaced older beliefs. But Christian monks in Ireland helped preserve Celtic culture in two ways. First, they incorporated swirling Celtic designs into religious works such as the Book of Kells. Christian themes blended with curving patterns from Celtic art.

Second, in about the eighth century, Irish monks wrote down old Celtic legends. Until then, the myths had been preserved by word of mouth. The myths help us understand what the Celts themselves believed—and not what other people say they believed. The myths and stories were gathered into several collections. The Irish Ulster Cycle recounts the adventures

The Book of Kells, created in an Irish monastery in the eighth century, uses a style of scrollwork based on Celtic designs to decorate the Bible.

of the hero Cú Chulainn, while the Fenian Cycle tells of Finn MacCool.

Legendary hero

In Wales, meanwhile, a collection of tales named the *Mabinogion* includes the legend of King Arthur. Scholars believe that the hero may be based on a real Celtic king who fought the Saxons in about A.D. 500. Some parts of the Arthur story are probably made up, like the round table at which his knights sat or the magical sword Excalibur. The king doesn't even play a big role in the *Mabinogion*. But many people believe Arthur's court, Camelot, was located at Tintagel in Cornwall, where the ruins of a castle cling to a steep crag. Archaeologists are not convinced: The jury's still out.

Celtic revival

Nearly 2,000 years after the Celts lost political power, their influence remains. There has been a revival of languages such as Welsh, Gaelic, and Breton. Place-names, too, echo the Celts: the rivers Seine, Danube, Rhine, and Thames have names derived from Celtic languages. The name of Belgium comes from a tribe called the Belgae, and that of Paris from the Parisii.

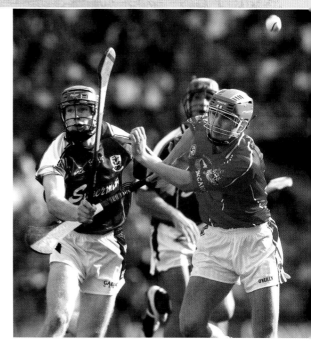

Hurling, a tough sport played mainly in Ireland, claims to be based on a Celtic game.

In Ireland and Scotland, the sports of hurling and shinty claim Celtic origins. Celtic music and dancing is revived at *ceilidhs*—a Gaelic word meaning parties—while music and poetry are celebrated at festivals such as the Welsh Eisteddfod. Today, many people in Europe, the United States, Canada, Australia, New Zealand, even Zimbabwe in southern Africa and Patagonia in South America, take a new pride in their Celtic heritage. And each Halloween children around the world get their costumes ready to celebrate the ancient festival of Samhain.

The Celtic cross is a Christian monument influenced by pre-Christian designs.

The Years Ahead

The late 20th century saw a revival of interest in all things Celtic. It also brought a surge of nationalism, or a desire for greater self-government in Wales, Scotland, Brittany, and Galicia. Many people in these Celtic lands see themselves as ethnic minorities. They believe that national governments do not do enough to help protect their distinctive culture.

Some nationalists use archaeology to support calls for independence, but this is often controversial. One debate surrounds the Stone of Scone, a block of stone said to have been taken to Scotland by Irish Celts. In 1296, the English king took it to London. It was incorporated into the base of a throne used during the coronation of British monarchs. In 1996, after calls from nationalists, the stone was returned to Scotland. But some scholars argue that it is not even Celtic. Similar controversy surrounds the numerous sites that are claimed to be Camelot, court of the Celtic King Arthur.

Archaeologists have an important role to play in such debates, as they sift the evidence to separate fact from fiction. As nationalist movements gain ground in Britain, France, and other areas, archaeologists will have their work cut out for years to come.

▽ **An actor dressed as the magician Merlin, from the court of King Arthur, poses in a cave at Tintagel, one of the suggested locations of Camelot.**

Glossary

amber – a hard yellow-brown material made from ancient tree resin and used to create objects such as jewelry

artifact – any object changed by human activity

assimilate – to adopt the ways of life of another people or culture

boss – a raised stud in the middle of a shield or other object

ceramics – objects made from clay and fired at high temperatures

circa – about; used to indicate a date that is approximate, and abbreviated as ca

earthwork – a bank, ditch, or other structure made from earth, usually to create a defensive position

economy – the way a people make a living, or the system by which they make and distribute wealth through the production and exchange of goods

elite – those who occupy the highest ranks in a society

embalm – to treat a dead body to prevent it from decaying

empire – a large area in which different territories or peoples are ruled by an emperor

equinox – when the sun is directly above the Equator and day and night are the same length all over the Earth; there are two equinoxes every year, in March and September

geometric – a pattern based on geometric shapes such as squares, circles, and rectangles

hillfort – a defended position on top of a hill

hoard – a hidden store

infrared – operating at wavelengths that are invisible to the human eye

ore – a natural stone that contains a metal such as iron that can be separated and used to make tools or weapons

pathologist – a scientist who studies the changes in a human body caused by disease or injury

peat – a soil-like material formed by decayed plants and burned as fuel

pilgrim – a person who makes a journey to a holy place in order to pray

ramparts – defensive walls built as barriers to attack

reconstruction – a modern attempt to make something in the same way as ancient peoples

relief – a sculpture that is raised from a flat surface

rituals – repeated practices that relate to specific, often religious, ceremonies

sack – to plunder a town after capturing it

shrine – a sacred place where people worship a god or a saint

sickle – a short-handled curved blade used to cut vegetation

siege – a military blockade to force a fort or town to surrender

sinew – a tendon that holds together bones in an animal's body

Stone Age – the first known period in human development when stone tools were used

survey – a careful collection of data about an area or subject

torque – a type of neckring worn by various ancient peoples

urn – a small jar with a lid

Bibliography

Books

The Celts: Europe's People of Iron (Lost Civilizations series). Alexandria, VA: Time-Life Books, 1994.

Collis, John. *The Celts: Origins, Myths, Inventions*. Stroud, UK: Tempus, 2003.

Green, Miranda. *Celtic World*. New York: Routledge, 1995.

James, Simon. *The Atlantic Celts: Ancient People or Modern Invention?* Madison: University of Wisconsin Press, 1999.

Articles

Biel, Jorg. "Treasure from a Celtic Tomb." NATIONAL GEOGRAPHIC (March 1980): 428–438.

O'Neill, Tom. "Celt Appeal." NATIONAL GEOGRAPHIC (March 2006): 74–95.

Severy, Merle. "The Celts." NATIONAL GEOGRAPHIC (May 1977): 582–633.

Further Reading

Cunliffe, Barry. *The Ancient Celts*. New York: Oxford University Press, 1997.

Grant, Neil. *Everyday Life of the Celts* (Uncovering History). North Mankato, MN: Smart Apple Media, 2003.

James, Simon. *The World of the Celts*. New York: Thames and Hudson, 1993.

Richardson, Hazel. *Life of the Ancient Celts* (People of the Ancient World). New York: Crabtree Publishing Company, 2005.

On the Web

BBC Wales Iron Age Celts page
http://www.bbc.co.uk/wales/celts/

Butser Ancient Farm
http://www.butser.org.uk/

e-Keltoi Journal of Interdisciplinary Celtic Studies
http://www.uwm.edu/Dept/celtic/ekeltoi/

Interactive History Resources: Celts and Romans
http://resourcesforhistory.com//

World of the Ancient Britons
http://www.gallica.co.uk/celts/contents.htm

Index

About the Author

JEN GREEN received a doctorate from the University of Sussex, United Kingdom, in 1982. She worked in publishing for 15 years and is now a full-time writer who has written more than 150 books for children on natural history, geography, the environment, history, and other subjects.

Sources for Quotations

Page 17 (Strabo, Diodorus Siculus): quoted in *The Celts, Europe's People of Iron.* Alexandria, VA: Time-Life Books, 1994.
Page 17 (Strabo, Ammanius Marcellinus): quoted in *Vanguard Magazine*, Number 116 (August-September 1996).
Page 18: Caesar, quoted in *Halloween Customs in the Ancient World,* Bettina Arnold, 2001.
Page 43: Carlos Alonso del Real, quoted in *La Prehistoria.* Pontevedra, Spain, 1991.

About the Consultant

BETTINA ARNOLD is professor of anthropology at the University of Wisconsin–Milwaukee, where she is also codirector of the Center for Celtic Studies. She specializes in the Iron Age culture of her native Germany and is the editor of *e-Keltoi*, an online interdisciplinary magazine of Celtic studies. Professor Arnold is particularly interested in gender roles in early societies, mortuary archaeology and what burials can tell us about past social structures, and the use and abuse of archaeology for political purposes in today's world.

> This bronze shield was decorated with studs of red glass. It was found in the Thames River in London, and may actually have been made to be thrown into the river as an offering to the river god.

One of the world's largest nonprofit scientific and educational organizations, the National Geographic Society was founded in 1888 "for the increase and diffusion of geographic knowledge." Fulfilling this mission, the Society educates and inspires millions every day through its magazines, books, television programs, videos, maps and atlases, research grants, the National Geographic Bee, teacher workshops, and innovative classroom materials. The Society is supported through membership dues, charitable gifts, and income from the sale of its educational products. This support is vital to National Geographic's mission to increase global understanding and promote conservation of our planet through exploration, research, and education.

For more information, please call 1-800-NGS-LINE (647-5463) or write to the following address:

National Geographic Society
1145 17th Street N.W.
Washington, D.C. 20036-4688
U.S.A.

Visit the Society's Web site:
www.nationalgeographic.com

Library of Congress Cataloging-in-Publication Data available upon request
Hardcover ISBN: 978-1-4263-0225-1
Library Edition ISBN: 978-1-4263-0226-8

Printed in Mexico

Series design by Jim Hiscott
The body text is set in Century Schoolbook.
The display text is set in Helvetica Neue, Clarendon.

National Geographic Society

John M. Fahey, Jr., *President and Chief Executive Officer;* Gilbert M. Grosvenor, *Chairman of the Board;* Nina D. Hoffman, *Executive Vice President, President of Book Publishing Group*

Staff for This Book

Nancy Laties Feresten, *Vice President, Editor-in-Chief of Children's Books*
Virginia Ann Koeth, *Project Editor*
Bea Jackson, *Director of Design and Illustration*
Jim Hiscott, *Art Director*
Lori Epstein, National Geographic Image Sales, *Illustrations Editors*
Jean Cantu, *Illustrations Specialist*
Priyanka Lamichhane, *Assistant Editor*
R. Gary Colbert, *Production Director*

Lewis R. Bassford, *Production Manager*
Maryclare Tracy, Nicole Elliott, *Manufacturing Managers*
Maps, *Mapping Specialists, Ltd.*

For the Brown Reference Group, plc
Tim Cooke, *Editor*
Alan Gooch, *Book Designer*
Laila Torsun, *Picture Researcher*
Encompass Graphics, *Cartographers*

Photo Credits
Front: Erich Lessing/Art Resource, N.Y.
Back: Erich Lessing/Art Resource, N.Y.
Spine: Mircea Bezergheanu/Shutterstock
Background: gds/zefa/Corbis
Icon: Bill McKelvie/Shutterstock

NGIC = National Geographic Image Collection; WFA = Werner Forman Archives
1, © Erich Lessing/Art Resource, N.Y.; 2–3, © Homer Sykes/Corbis; 4, © Michael St Maur Shell/Corbis; 6, © Mircea Bezergheanu/Shutterstock; 9, © Bettina Arnold 10, © Werner Forman/Corbis; 11 top, © National Museum, Ireland/WFA; 11 bottom, © Volkmar K. Wentzel/NGIC; 12–13, © The Scotsman/ Corbis; 14, © Lorthois/Corbis; 15, © Silkeborg Museum, Denmark/ WFA; 16, © Pasquale Sorrentino/Science Photo Library; 17, © British Museum, London/WFA; 18, © Musee de la Civilisation/Gallo-Romaine Lyon/Gianni Dagli Orti/Art Archive; 19 top, © Narodni Museum, Prague/WFA; 19 bottom, © Robert Clark/NGIC; 20, © Adam Hart-Davis/ Science Photo Library; 21, © British Museum, London/ WFA; 22–23, © Robert Clark/NGIC; 24, © Professor Niels Lynnerup/NGIC; 25 top, © Rober Clark/NGIC; 25 bottom, © Robert Clark/NGIC; 26, © Robert Clark/ NGIC; 27 top, © Robert Clark/NGIC; 27 bottom, © Robert Clark/NGIC; 28–29, © National Museum, Copenhagen/WFA; 30, © James P. Blair/ NGIC; 31 top, © National Museum, Copenhagen/WFA; 31 bottom; © James P. Blair/NGIC; 32, © Eye of Science/Science Photo Library; 33, © Jason Hawkes/ Corbis; 34 top, © WFA; 34 bottom, © WFA; 35, © British Museum, London/WFA; 36–37, © Volkmar K. Wentzel/NGIC; 38, © Lloyd Kenneth Townsend Jnr/NGIC; 39 top, © Volkmar K. Wentzel/ NGIC; 39 bottom, © Volkmar K. Wentzel/NGIC; 40, © AKG Images; 41, © Erich Lessing/ AKG Images; 42, © Archives CDA/Guillo/AKG Images; 43 top, © Werner Forman/Corbis; 43 bottom, © Siisie Brimberg/NGIC; 44–45, © Skyscan/Corbis; 46 top, © AKG Images; 46 bottom left, © AKG Images; 46 bottom right, © AKG Images; 47, © 20th Century Fox/Album/ AKG Images; 48, © British Museum, London/WFA; 49, © Roger Halls/Cordaly Picture Library Ltd/Corbis; 50, © Susanne Sievers; 51, © Susanne Sievers; 52–53, © Adam Woolfitt/Corbis; 54, © Araldo de Luca/Corbis; 55 © Leonard de Selva/Corbis; 56, © AKG Images; 57 top, © Empics/Topham; 57 bottom, © Stephen Aaaron Rees/Shutterstock; 58, © Richard T. Nowitz/Corbis; 63, © British Museum, London/WFA

Front cover: Detail of the silver Gundestrup Cauldron showing a Celtic god with two stags.
Page 1 and back cover: A bronze statuette of a white boar made sometime between the sixth and first centuries B.C. and discovered in Liechtenstein.
Pages 2–3: The British Camp, one of two neighboring Iron Age hillforts near Malvern in southern Britain.

NATIONAL GEOGRAPHIC
OGRAPHIC INVESTIGAG
NVESTIGATES NATIONAL
ES NATIONAL GEOGRAPH
GEOGRAPHIC INVESTIG
C INVESTIGATES NATION
ATES NATIONAL GEOGRA
NAL GEOGRAPHIC INVEST
PHIC INVESTIGATES NAT
GATES NATIONAL GEOG
ONAL GEOGRAPHIC INVE
RAPHIC INVESTIGATES N
STIGATES NATIONAL GEO
ATIONAL GEOGRAPHIC I
OGRAPHIC INVESTIGATE
NVESTIGATES NATIONAL
S NATIONAL GEOGRAPHI